GREENHOUSE
GARDENING

CHANCELLOR
PRESS

Acknowledgements

This book has been compiled with material previously published
by Reed International Books.

Text by Richard Rosenfeld. Additional text by Meg Sanders.
Illustrations by Vicky Emptage. Symbols by Coryn Dickman.

The publishers would like to thank the following organizations and
individuals for their kind permission to reproduce the photographs
in this book:
Alton Greenhouses, 13; A-Z Botanical Collection 29; Michael Boys 27; Eric
Crichton Photos 28, 32, 37, 45, 46, 48, 49, 50, 51, 53, 54, 57, 63, 65, 66, 69;
Jerry Harpur 24; Neil Holmes 25, 36, 40, 41, 55, 62; John Moss 47; Photos
Horticultural 35, 64; Reed International Books Ltd/Michael Boys 22, 26, 33,
44/M. Crockett 11/Jerry Harpur 23, 39, 42, 56, 58, 59, 61/Neil Holmes 72;
Harry Smith Collection 30, 34, 71; Peter Stiles 38, 43, 52, 60, 67, 68, 73;
Judy Todd 70; George Wright 31.

First published in Great Britain in 1995
by Chancellor Press, an imprint of Reed Consumer Books Limited
Michelin House, 81 Fulham Road, London SW3 6RB
and Auckland, Melbourne, Singapore and Toronto

© 1995 Reed International Books Limited

ISBN 1 85152 625 0

A catalogue record for this book is available from the British Library

Produced by Mandarin Offset, Hong Kong
Printed in Hong Kong

CONTENTS

INTRODUCTION

A greenhouse is rarely among the initial purchases made by the novice gardener. Sometimes a house move will provide one as an unexpected bonus, and this then provides the impetus for exploring what the possibilities of greenhouse gardening really are. But more often, a greenhouse comes way down the shopping list, well after the lawnmower and the investment in a stainless steel spade. It can take a few years of gardening before a greenhouse becomes a priority, but once it does, nothing else will really do.

Sooner or later, you may start to feel that the only logical solution to your garden problem is to buy a glasshouse. It could be that the trays of seedlings are filling the spare room, or that two cold winters in a row have blasted treasured specimen plants, or that the vegetables did not get an early enough start to crop fully before early frosts, or that the cost of stocking hanging baskets with bought-in half-hardy plants has become prohibitive, or quite simply that you have taken a fancy to tender plants that will just not survive outdoors. But whatever your expectations, they will almost certainly be exceeded once the greenhouse comes on line.

Generally, even before acquiring a greenhouse, you will have started to provide some weather protection by buying a cold frame and a few cloches, and these will remain a useful adjunct to the greenhouse, for hardening-off and soil-warming. But even if you initially rejected buying a greenhouse because of limited space, it is worth taking another look at what is available. Since the designs have become ever more ingenious and space saving, there is a structure to fit almost any space, aspect and pocket. If space and money are not limiting factors, however, the sky is the limit. There are wonderful, elaborate structures available, as decorative as they are functional, but even the simplest greenhouse will make a tremendous difference to the repertoire of plants and techniques available to you.

CHOOSING AND USING In a temperate climate, conditions can vary hugely from year to year and even usually mild, coastal areas can suddenly suffer from frost or lashing salt-laden winds. The most experienced gardener can do little to avoid these damaging and sometimes disastrous weather effects and in a really bad year, entire crops can be wiped out or spoiled. With a glasshouse, you can create an environment where extremes are controlled. Drought need not affect your plants and heavy rain or even hail early in the season is no longer a worry. The damaging effects of late or early frosts can be avoided and even scorching summer sun can be mitigated, by incorporating ventilation and shading.

The repertoire of plants that can be propagated, forced and grown is enormously extended by even the simplest glasshouse. Winter protection for half-hardy plants is the first advantage that springs to mind, but using a greenhouse to gain a precious few weeks' advance when growing annual ornamentals, and crops such as French beans, outdoor tomatoes, leeks and onions or even carrots, can greatly improve results by effectively extending the growing season. Combined with simple soil-warming polypropylene fleece or cloches, you can gain weeks of extra growing time.

Tender ornamentals, and crops such as glasshouse tomatoes, aubergines, peppers and melons can only be grown with a greenhouse. Not even the best system of cloches and lights could cope with plants such as perpetual carnations, orchids or melons, or trained standard fuchsias or bays. Once you have used your greenhouse for these rather more ambitious projects, there is really no going back.

Choosing a greenhouse is a difficult process, particularly if you have never used one. It is hard to imagine the kind of use you will be putting it to in, say, five years' time and finding the balance between a greenhouse that will allow you to extend your use as time goes by and one that is simply over-ambitious for your requirements is quite a delicate task.

Most people start with an unheated greenhouse, and add the heating later. Although it's generally assumed that the cold greenhouse will be limiting, it's surprising how useful it can be. You can grow many of the same crops and ornamental plants as in a heated greenhouse, only you can't start so early in the year. You must wait for nature to provide the higher temperatures. You can also grow frost-tender plants such as fuchsias and tuberous begonias, provided you keep them in the greenhouse only from late spring to early autumn. Thereafter raise indoors on a windowsill.

The heated greenhouse extends the growing season, keeping tomatoes fruiting until near Christmas, which is out of the question in an unheated greenhouse in cold regions. It also enables you to bring 'tender perennials' into the warmth over winter. The term is partly relative and depends upon where you live. In mild, sheltered, protected gardens by the Gulf Stream you can probably leave an *Osteospermum* 'Buttermilk' outside all year round. But in an exposed chilly site the plant might die without winter protection.

PARAFFIN HEATERS They are more expensive to run than they used to be, but at least they are more sophisticated, with many models specifically manufactured for the greenhouse. They are essentially a plant 'life-saver', being used when the temperature gets close to freezing. However, there are two disadvantages. Firstly, you must have the time to light and turn them off. Secondly, you might decide to leave the heater running on a freezing morning but not be around later in the day to switch it off when the weather improves and the greenhouse temperature soars to high levels.

Paraffin heaters are a means of keeping the greenhouse frost-free in the winter months. Even though they have their disadvantages, any form of heating extends the growing season as outside temperatures drop.

GAS HEATERS They are far more convenient, being available with thermostatic controls. Some run off the mains but they are usually more expensive than those needing gas cylinders. The advantage of both paraffin and gas is that you don't have to go to the expense of installing electricity.

ELECTRICITY This is the most reliable and economical form of heating. By using an accurate thermostat the heat is only on when you need it, and cuts out the moment the required temperature is reached. Also, electric heaters automatically switch themselves off and on. The one worry of course is a power cut, which is most likely in the severest winter weather. It pays to have a paraffin heater in reserve.

HEATING LEVELS Greenhouses may be classified according to the temperature to which one is prepared to heat them. In this book, four levels of heating are considered:

		Temperature range
1	The cool greenhouse	5-7°C (40-45°F)
2	The intermediate greenhouse sub-divided into:	
	a) gentle heat	7 13°C (45 55°F)
	b) warm heat	13-18°C (55-65°F)
3	The tropical greenhouse	min. 18°C (65°F)

In the latter part of the book (p.21 onwards) you will find a carefully selected range of greenhouse plants, arranged alphabetically, and grouped according to the above four temperature levels.

GREENHOUSE SELECTION

When you've decided how much space you can allot to a greenhouse, and the range of plants to be grown, examine the different types for design, material, covering, size, and heating.

DESIGN This means either lean-to or free-standing. The former has the benefit of extra, natural heat when a glass side is replaced by a heat-retaining wall. Furthermore if the lean-to encloses the back door of the house it traps escaping heat and invariably guarantees a frost-free winter. The disadvantage is that even when built against a warm, sunny wall the lean-to is in the shade for at least part of the day. This is not ideal for growing tomatoes, or propagation.

Provided the free-standing greenhouse is sensibly sited it automatically receives more light. Manufacturers have recently become more inventive and now provide circular versions in addition to the traditional rectangular shape. Some have attractive domed roofs and make fine, albeit expensive, garden features.

The lean-to and free-standing greenhouse can be either glass from ground to roof, or have a waist-high lower section. The former lets in more light (vital for growing vegetables in the border), the latter provides extra insulation and is the better option for growing flowering plants. Pots can be stood on the bench, with bulbs, bags of soil, etc., stored beneath during winter.

MATERIAL Aluminium greenhouses are cheaper to buy but can be quite an eye-sore, whereas the red/brown cedar wood could not look better. It's mainly a question of cost, though the aluminium bars do tend to be slightly narrower than wooden ones and let in more light. Wood, on the other hand, is marginally more efficient at retaining heat. It's also much easier for putting up shelves where you want them; you don't have to drill holes in the metal. Just occasionally though the wood does need treating with wood preservative to retain colour and prevent rotting.

COVERING The main alternative is plastic, as in the

mobile polythene tunnel. You can site it over one part of the vegetable garden in early spring and treat it as a giant cloche; then use elsewhere, all summer long, for tomatoes etc.; and finally stand over a late-season fruiting crop. The main problem is the more it's moved, the greater the likelihood of torn plastic. It is generally reckoned that the covering won't last more than three or four years before running repairs, or a complete replacement, are required.

If your conventional greenhouse is packed to the limit then the polythene tunnel is an excellent way of creating extra inexpensive room.

SIZE Quite simply, the bigger the better. Not only do small greenhouses overheat in mid-summer, but they nearly always limit your ambitions. And once you've got a greenhouse those ambitions multiply. Two tomato plants, five seed trays, and a handful of tender, ornamental plants might initially seem fine, but when you see the results and start wanting to compare five different tomato varieties and grow ever more exotic plants then you'll certainly regret your decision. You shouldn't need anything larger than 2.7 x 3.3m/9 x 11ft size, though in most cases 1.8 x 2.4m/6 x 8ft is adequate. In any event ensure you buy the kind of greenhouse on which you can build extensions.

POSITION AND SITE

In a very small garden you won't have much choice where to site the greenhouse. It goes in the only available space. But if you do have a choice, you must apply certain important criteria.

LIGHT Place the greenhouse so that one end points to the rising sun, the other to the setting sun. Since the sun's path varies from summer to winter chose a line between the two extremes, guaranteeing maximum sunlight throughout the year.

This also means standing the greenhouse well away from shade cast by trees and buildings (not least to avoid damage from falling branches and dislodged roof slates), though some degree of shelter is necessary. Vulnerable sites can be improved by a wind-filtering hedge planted at a distance of three times the greenhouse height on the most exposed side. Nearby walls are not a good idea since they force the prevailing wind over and down, resulting in damaging turbulence.

SPADE WORK Preparing the foundation site involves making it level and uniformly firm. Many metal greenhouses now have pre-formed bases which are easily assembled. The base is set on top of the prepared soil with the greenhouse being bolted in place. If you don't buy the manufacturer's base, build a dwarf wall about three bricks high and assemble the greenhouse on top. Whether choosing brick or metal, it is essential the base is level from side to side, front to back, and across both diagonals. Always use a spirit level.

Before constructing the greenhouse lay out all the parts. Use a felt-tip pen to label each piece so you can see what it is and where it goes according to the plan. Assemble the structure flat on the ground, each side constructed in turn before being bolted to the base. The glazing bars in the roof are normally inserted last. Allow a complete day for assembling, and another day to glaze. Don't attempt the latter when you've only two more available hours because if left unfinished the structure can be damaged by the wind.

MAINTENANCE Twice a year give the greenhouse a

thorough clean. Once in the autumn, before tender plants are put under glass, and once in early spring before seed sowing begins. Having emptied the area scrub the frame, glass, staging, shelves, and floor if it's concrete, with hot water and detergent. Scrape off any moss or algae growing on the glass, and ensure no cracks appear between the sections of glass. Finally, rinse down with a strong jet from the hose pipe, and leave open the doors and ventilators to let the greenhouse dry. It's crucial to clean out any stacks of plant pots to eliminate pests and diseases, and to store them away on a shelf.

The second task involves preparing the borders for planting. Fork them over, and dig in plenty of peat, well-rotted manure or garden compost to improve the soil. Rake the soil level, and remove any large stones, dead leaves and other debris. There is no need to add fertilizer before planting or sowing in the autumn. However you should add a sprinkling of Growmore two weeks before a spring sowing.

BASIC EQUIPMENT

VENTILATORS Whenever the sun comes out the temperature inside the greenhouse rises sharply. But while plants like warmth, too much heat quickly dries them out and can be fatal. Ventilation keeps temperatures down to acceptable levels, enabling plants to thrive. Ideally you should keep the temperature below 27°C/81°F, though provided plants are well-watered they should be able to withstand slightly higher temperatures for brief periods.

Most greenhouses are equipped with a single ventilator in the roof. This is usually adequate, provided you are in constant attendance. If not, use an automatic appliance. They contain a special tube of paraffin wax which expands or contracts with a rise or fall in the temperature, extending or shortening a rod which in turn opens and closes the ventilator. Make certain that your model can support the required weight. The minimum is easily ascertained by resting the open window on a pair of household scales.

SHADING During mid-summer even good ventilation is inadequate at reducing the highest temperatures. Seedlings wilt and are sun-scorched. To overcome such problems shade the greenhouse. You can paint the outside with a special liquid, or attach protective 'bubble' sheeting within.

STAGING For maximum ventilation and humidity use corrugated iron sheets with holes drilled in to drain away water, and a short surrounding rim. Pour horticultural grit within, where the plant pots stand. The alternative is wooden slatted tables, which it must be said look much more attractive, and are far more easily purchased. However they're not much use for automatic watering systems. And plants dry out faster as the air whips through the gaps.

POTS They come in various sizes, such as 9cm/3½in, the figure denoting the distance across the top. Clay pots are useful for large, top-heavy plants, especially if they are going to stand outside over summer. Their weight reduces the risk of their being blown over.

When using clay pots, in the greenhouse, note that modern

greenhouse staging is rarely sufficiently sturdy to take the weight of too many heavy containers. This weight is enormously increased when the soil within has been watered. Staging is mainly designed to support plastic pots, whose chief virtue is their cheapness and ability to hold water (which is absorbed by clay).

SEED TRAYS The polypropylene kind are the easiest, being easy to wash and virtually indestructible. Wooden trays used to be popular but they rot, break, and need to be scrubbed hard when cleaned. Yoghurt pots, plastic mushroom boxes and margarine tubs make excellent alternatives.

AUTOMATIC WATERING If you are out a lot use an automatic watering device. They usually involve a tank of water hanging from the greenhouse roof from which plastic tubes leak water into pots or border soil. All you need do is top up the tank.

An alternative is capillary matting which is laid across the staging beneath the plant pots. The tubes leak water onto the mat and the plants draw up all the moisture they require. You can make your own version in which you omit the water bag and tubes, and instead soak the matting each morning.

PLANT CULTIVATION

COMPOST Special compost for pot plants is required because the food content, drainage and oxygenating qualities of garden soil are unsuitable for container plants. The compost tends to be either peat or soil based. The latter are called John Innes and come in three grades, Nos 1-3, depending on whether they have twice or three times as much nutrient as No 1.

Generally, plants in pots up to 10cm/4in take No 1; 10-17cm/4-7in take No 2; plants in larger containers take No 3. Peat-based composts are not graded like this; you must read the manufacturer's comments to determine their nutrient value.

FEEDING Compost nutrients last approximately three months before they're used up or washed out. You must there-fore replace them with an all-purpose liquid or solid feed over the growing period. Such feed contains a balanced diet of nitrogen (promoting foliage), potassium (for good flowers), and phosphorous (fruit ripening and root development). Provide liquid feed to keep pace with a plant's increasing growing requirements (eg tomatoes); solid, slow-release feed is useful if you are regularly away. It is important to feed only during the growing season. If practised at any other time you produce lanky growth and considerably weaken the plant.

POTTING ON When a plant becomes root-bound move up into the next size pot. Remove the plant from its existing con-tainer by putting the fingers of one hand across the surface, turning it upside down, and tapping the rim on the work sur-face. The plant should easily slide out. Cut back any really long roots level with the root-ball and remove some surface compost. Next put a handful of broken crocks, curved side up, into the bottom of the new container for efficient drainage and fill the sides and top with compost. Finally water in.

POTTING BULBS When dealing with bulbs and corms let them die down naturally after flowering, dry off and rest, and then repot them in the same size container (or one a little larg-er), with fresh compost. Discard the old compost, and remove withered roots, though only partially if new white ones are evi-dent. They must not, under any circumstances, be damaged.

PROPAGATION

In 99 per cent of cases propagating is child's play. It either involves seed sowing or taking cuttings. Generally, dahlia, delphinium etc, are propagated in early spring allowing the new plants to flower that summer; plants with corms are propagated several weeks later; and geraniums, fuchsias, etc, are increased in late summer so they can root before the winter.

TIP CUTTINGS These are immature non-flowering shoot tips. Many perennials and sub-shrubs are increased in this way. Make a sharp cut just below a node and remove the bottom pair of leaves before placing the cutting in the rooting medium. Sometimes it is best to take a cutting with a heel, as described below. Soft cuttings take 10-30 days to take root.

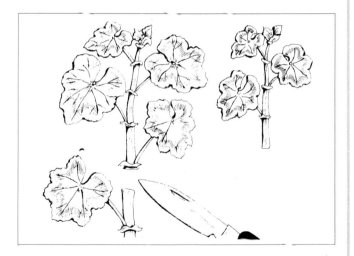

SEMI-RIPE CUTTINGS These are firmer than soft cuttings. They are usually taken in summer and do not need added heat; a cold frame is the best environment. Take a cutting from a healthy side shoot of a shrub, if necessary with a heel (ie attached to a slither of older wood at the base). Cleanly remove the soft tip and the lowest pair of leaves before inserting in the rooting medium. Keep the frame closed and spray on warm days to keep moist. The cutting should make a fine young plant the following spring. Any that have not rooted should be discarded.

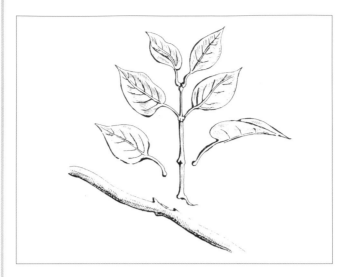

DIVISION Most perennials are increased by division, and some need dividing from time to time if they become over-crowded. Lift the plant when dormant – between autumn and spring. Separate the sections by hand, trowel or two forks *(below)* in the case of larger plants. Discard the central, woody sections and replant the outer parts. Tough crowns should be washed free of soil and the sections cut up with a sharp knife. Make sure each part has roots and buds before replanting.

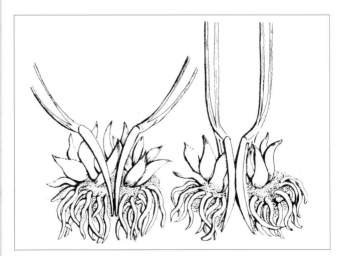

A-Z OF GREENHOUSE PLANTS

1 COOL
2 INTERMEDIATE
- GENTLE
- WARM
3 TROPICAL

KEY TO SYMBOLS

GROW IN GREENHOUSE BED OR BORDER (B)	GROW IN CONTAINER (C)	GROW IN GREENHOUSE BED, BORDER OR CONTAINER (B/C)	PERIOD WHEN IN FLOWER /SPATHE APPEARS
PREFFERED POSITION	MAXIMUM HEIGHT	MAXIMUM SPREAD	DEGREE OF HARDINESS
GREENHOUSE TEMPERATURE- COOL/GENTLE /WARM/TROPICAL	DEGREE OF PRUNING NECESSARY	RECOMMENDED SHAPE	HARVEST TIME
SOWING OR PLANTING DEPTH	DISTANCE BETWEEN PLANTS	GROWING TIME	EVERGREEN

ABUTILON

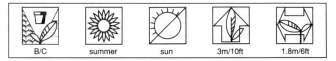

| B/C | summer | sun | 3m/10ft | 1.8m/6ft |

The genus includes hardy and half-hardy flowering shrubs which range in size from slender, elegant climbers to small shrubby plants. The tender varieties need frost protection over winter, but should be stood outdoors for the summer. They flower in a good range of bold and subtle colours such as white, yellow, blue, with *A. megapotamicum* 'Variegatum' *(above)* offering green leaves splashed with cream.

GROWING Provide stony, free-draining soil in sunny or dappled shade. If growing in containers use 25cm/10in pots of John Innes No 2. Water generously over summer, sparingly over winter. Floppy stems need to be tied to canes, or against a trellis.

PROPAGATION Take cuttings of 7.5cm/3in side shoots in late spring. Raise in a heated propagator at a temperature of 18°C/65°F.

SPECIES *A. striatum* 'Thompsonii' has mottled variegated leaves and orange bell-like flowers. It'll reach 1.2m/4ft high in a pot. *A. × hybridum* 'Kentish Belle' has similar flowers to *megapotamicum*, but grows slightly smaller at 2.4m/8ft.

POSSIBLE PROBLEMS Whitefly; mealy bugs. It can look

CHOISYA

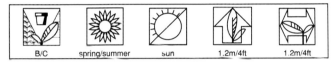

| B/C | spring/summer | sun | 1.2m/4ft | 1.2m/4ft |

Choisya, the Mexican orange, can be grown in most gardens given a sheltered position, or better still in ornamental pots and pruned for shape as in the Mediterranean. The small, white, star-shaped flowers open for about two weeks in spring and release the most fantastic scent, sufficient to fill an entire greenhouse.

GROWING Provide well drained soil and John Innes No 3 for large, pot-grown specimens. Stand in full sunlight.

PROPAGATION Easily increase by taking 10cm/4in soft wood cuttings in late summer. Plant in a mix of peat and sand and maintain at 18°C/65°F. Pot up always into the next size container and stand outdoors in summer after hardening off.

VARIETIES *C. ternata (above)* grows to 1.2m/4ft in the open but can be kept smaller in a pot. It has glossy dark green leaves which release a fragrant smell when torn and crushed. *C.t.* 'Sundance' has yellow variegated leaves. Both are capable of flowering intermittently through the summer and again in autumn, but don't count on it.

POSSIBLE PROBLEMS Generally trouble-free.

CHRYSANTHEMUM

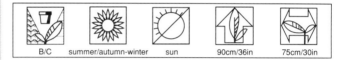

| B/C | summer/autumn-winter | sun | 90cm/36in | 75cm/30in |

Chrysanthemums are a large group of plants categorized primarily according to their flowering period. The late-flowerers can bloom as late as Christmas. They are grown in pots kept outside over summer and brought under glass in late autumn so the blooms aren't ruined by the frost.

GROWING Container-grown perennials should be potted up in 9cm/3½in pots. Initially water sparingly, giving just enough to prevent the plants from wilting. Later, pinch out the growing tips at least twice for extra bushiness and increase the watering. As the plants put on good growth commence feeding and tie in to a cane. For the final potting up use John Innes No 3. When the plants are brought back into the greenhouse in autumn, ventilate to avoid botrytis.

PROPAGATION When all the flowers have been cut, prune back the stems and store in the greenhouse. Pot up in peat in late winter and increase heat to promote growth. When shoots appear take cuttings 10cm/4in long and root them in seed compost at 16°C/60°F.

VARIETIES There are scores to chose from, including 'Autumn Days' (bronze, early autumn flowering), 'Peter Rowe' (yellow, early autumn), 'Green Satin' (green, late autumn) and the intermediate decorative varieties *(above)*.

POSSIBLE PROBLEMS Earwigs can be a major nuisance.

DIANTHUS

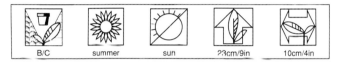

| B/C | summer | sun | 23cm/9in | 10cm/4in |

While dianthus, or carnations, can easily be grown outdoors certain kinds make excellent greenhouse specimen plants, and are unbeatable for their rich, perfumed fragrance.

GROWING Dwarf varieties can be grown in 13cm/5in pots of John Innes No 2. For tall, stylish specimens plant 12 per grow-bag at a distance of 15cm/6in, or alternatively in individual terracotta pots. Cane support is essential to prevent them flopping over. Only the central bud of each shoot should be allowed to develop if large blooms are required. Water lightly and trim back after flowering to avoid straggly growth. For border carnations pinch out regularly for bushiness.

PROPAGATION Take 10cm/4in cuttings in spring and summer. Pot up into 7.5cm/3in pots of John Innes No 1. Alternatively raise from seed at a temperature of 18°C/65°F.

VARIETIES 'Mrs Sinkins' is a cottage garden favourite. It has white flowers and strong scent. Also good for fragrance are 'Pink Jewel', pink; 'Sops-in-Wine', maroon.

POSSIBLE PROBLEMS Leaf rot in winter.

ECHEVERIA

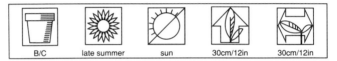

| B/C | late summer | sun | 30cm/12in | 30cm/12in |

Olive grey succulents which consist of neat circles of waxy leaves, building up to a 30cm/12in mound in the largest species. In late summer they send up long pole-like stems with flame yellow-orange-red flowers. Eye-catching.

GROWING Start off in small pots with John Innes No 1 and, later, No 2. Free-drainage is essential. Over winter little water is necessary, and when feeding avoid spilling drops into the rosette because they quickly stain. Accidents can be tackled by fiercely blowing away the water. If too many of the plant's lower leaves shrivel and wither, slice off the top in spring and plant up.

PROPAGATION In spring cut away the offsets with a sharp knife. Some may have minuscule root systems. If not it doesn't matter. Dip the soft, fleshy bottom in rooting powder and plant up. It will quickly settle.

SPECIES *E. × derenosa* 'Warfield Wonder' is easily grown, flowering in orange and yellow. *E. derenbergii* has orange flowers and freely produces offsets. *E. setosa*, the Mexican firecracker, is shown above.

POSSIBLE PROBLEMS Beware of overwatering.

FIG

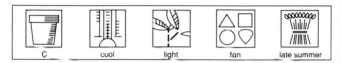

| C | cool | light | fan | late summer |

Specimens don't have to grow big to provide fruit. When a container grown plant reaches the height of 90cm/36in, it will produce a perfectly decent crop. While you can use outdoor varieties ('Brown Turkey'), those specifically for the greenhouse ('White Marseilles' and 'Rouge de Bordeaux') yield better quality fruit. The height of a mature specimen should be approximately 3m/10ft x 4.5m/15ft.

GROWING In spring select a bushy young plant. Transfer to a larger container, if pot-bound, filled with John Innes No 3. Give minimum amounts of water until several new leaves appear, and then increase. Prune in winter only to remove damaged shoots and prevent excessive overcrowding. By the time figs appear on the shoot tips the plant will need quite heavy watering, particularly on hot days when up to 4.5 litres / 1 gallon will be required. If you let the soil dry out the fruit will fall. After harvesting the leaves fall and watering virtually ceases.

HARVESTING Pick the fruit when very soft; it should easily come away from the tree. Note that a crop ripens over a four- to six-week period.

POSSIBLE PROBLEMS Botrytis on young shoots leads to die-back. The fungus can also attack the fruit which will then rot or fall prematurely.

FREESIA

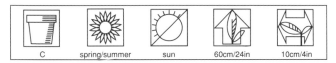

| C | spring/summer | sun | 60cm/24in | 10cm/4in |

F. × kewensis 'Everest' *(above)* is perfect for greenhouse scent and colour. Packets of corms are usually bought as single or double mixed hybrids.

GROWING Plant the corms from autumn to spring, with six per 12.5cm/5in pot, each covered by 2.5cm/1in of John Innes No 2. Insert canes for tying in, and water. Thereafter wait until the foliage starts to grow. Keep pots outside until there's a hint of frost and then bring them under glass and keep at a minimum of 5°C/40°F. Autumn-planted corms should flower the following spring. From the time flowering commences reduce watering to a bare minimum and cut for an indoor vase. When the foliage dies down decrease watering. Keep the corms dry in a cool, bright place until the autumn.

PROPAGATION Freesias propagate themselves at the rate of 2:1 per season. Detach offsets when removing the corms from their pots and that autumn plant up the same-size bulbs together. Offsets may not flower until they've reached a good size in their second year.

VARIETIES Named varieties are usually hard to find.

POSSIBLE PROBLEMS Generally trouble-free.

FUCHSIA

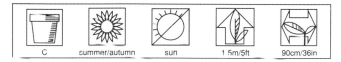

| C | summer/autumn | sun | 1.5m/5ft | 90cm/36in |

The first fuchsias were discovered by a missionary in the Americas in 1703. Today there are hundreds of varieties, most of them tender. They can be kept outside through the summer but need to be kept under glass over the winter.

GROWING Younger plants will only survive the winter in a warm greenhouse. Alternatively use a windowsill. In late autumn prune back the main branch by half and water gently in a pot refilled with John Innes No 2. Spray with fungicide to prevent attacks of botrytis. In an unheated greenhouse prune back hard, and reduce watering more significantly. Do not let the soil dry out totally or the plant will die. Provide artificial heat to keep temperatures just above freezing. Recommence regular watering in spring as the plant puts on growth.

PROPAGATION Take young shoot cuttings, 7.5cm/3in long, in spring or summer. Pot up in a 9cm/3½in pot and maintain at 16°C/61°F. Since the best flowers come from young plants take cuttings every other year.

CULTIVARS 'Checkerboard' has bright red and white flowers. 'Dark Eyes', red and violet-blue flowers; 'Lady Kathleen Spence', white and pale pink flowers. 'Thalia' *(above)* has long, red flowers. 'Stanley Cash' is ideal for a hanging basket because it produces a cascade of flowers in white and red.

POSSIBLE PROBLEMS Whitefly; rust.

29

GLADIOLUS

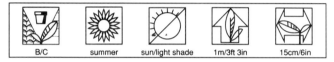

| B/C | summer | sun/light shade | 1m/3ft 3in | 15cm/6in |

Most gladioli bulbs are half-hardy and need to be lifted and stored over winter. Some, like *G. callianthus* (also known as *Acidanthera murielae; above*) are particularly refined and highly scented, and are worth growing in greenhouse tubs for an early display.

GROWING Plant corms of *G. c.* in late spring with a 15cm/6in covering of John Innes No 2. The bottom of the pot needs excellent drainage, and each bulb should sit on a sprinkling of horticultural sand. Initially water sparingly and increase with growth. In the autumn, after flowering, decrease watering as the foliage fades. Remove the stems and dry the corms in a cool, well-ventilated spot. Turn them upside down so all moisture can drain away. Store in muslin or netting.

PROPAGATION When the corms are lifted remove offsets and store with the parents. Plant out the following spring. Note offsets can take three years to flower. It is often easier to increase stock by purchasing new bulbs.

VARIETIES *G. c.* has pure white flowers with a purple splash deep inside the trumpet; height 1m/3ft 3in. *G. papilio* has hooded, yellow or white flowers; height 1.2m/4ft. *G. primulinus* also has hooded, creamy-yellow flowers; height 60cm/24in.

POSSIBLE PROBLEMS Core, and dry rot; leaf spot; scab.

HYACINTHUS

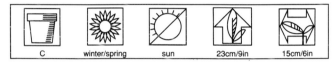

C	winter/spring	sun	23cm/9in	15cm/6in

All the garden-grown and pot-raised hyacinths are related to *H. orientalis*. The earliest to bloom are the Roman hyacinths (at Christmas), with others flowering into late spring. The fragrance is exquisite.

GROWING Plant mid-winter flowering bulbs in early autumn. Place one in a 10cm/4in pot, or allow 2.5cm/1in between bulbs. Cover to the tip with John Innes No 2 and only lightly press in. Water, place in a dark cupboard, and keep at a temperature of 5°C/40°F. Bring out when there's 2.5cm/1in of growth and gradually increase both light and heat. After flowering, cut off the flowering stem and feed until the foliage fades. Then store the bulbs until the autumn, and plant outside.

PROPAGATION Increase by seed and leave undisturbed until they are at least one year old, then plant up. Note that it can take three years for the bulbs to flower. Offsets are possible but they are rare, and as with seed the quality is not guaranteed. Propagation is best left to the special techniques of professional nurserymen.

VARIETIES 'Delft Blue' is particularly highly scented. 'Jan Boss' is red. 'Lady Derby', pink. 'L'Innocence', white and 'Pink Pearl' *(above)* is deep pink.

POSSIBLE PROBLEMS Grey bulb rot; aphids; storage rot.

31

MIMULUS

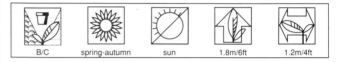

| B/C | spring-autumn | sun | 1.8m/6ft | 1.2m/4ft |

Grow mimulus, the monkey flower, for strident greenhouse colour – crimsons, sharp-yellows, orange. Some species are herbaceous perennials, preferring permanently damp soil, others make very good pot plants. The taller kinds are perfect for training up a wall or pillar.

GROWING Provide a rich soil, John Innes No 3 with a regular summer feed. In spring repot, and prune for shape and size. Water liberally throughout the summer. Cut back flowering stems in the autumn.

PROPAGATION Take spring and summer cuttings, 10cm/ 4in long, and raise in a mix of sand and peat. Later move to a small pot of John Innes No 1. Alternatively, germinate seed at 15°C/60°F.

SPECIES *M. glutinosus* grows to 1.8m/6ft and has orange flowers, pink round the lips of the tube; free-flowering. It is sometimes listed as *Diplacus glutinosus*. *M. luteus*, monkey musk, has yellow flowers with maroon blotches. *M. moschatus (above)* is a dwarf species, reaching 25cm/10in.

POSSIBLE PROBLEMS Generally trouble-free.

PEACH/NECTARINE

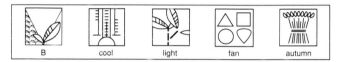

| B | cool | light | fan | autumn |

Though they are hardy enough to be grown outdoors, the best yield comes from plants grown under glass where there's guaranteed warmth. Use a lean-to against a sunny wall. Height 3m/10ft x 3m/10ft.

GROWING Plant over winter 30cm/12in away from the wall in extremely well drained, fertile soil. Lean the stem back so it can grow and be trained up a criss-cross of wires against the wall. Two weeks before planting add a scattering of general fertilizer. Thereafter add Growmore each spring. Train as a fan shape. More general pruning can only be carried out after late spring to avoid infection. For an early supply of fruit do not ventilate from early spring (unless temperatures exceed 15°C/60°F). Pollinate by hand, preferably at mid-day, and always maintain a moderately humid atmosphere by damping down. Thin the emerging fruitlets to three per cluster, and later to a distance of 15cm/6in.

HARVESTING Pick when plump and ripe. The fruit should easily come away if given a gentle, twisting tug.

POSSIBLE PROBLEMS Red spider mite. It helps to clean and whitewash the walls each (or every alternate) winter, untying the web of stems and easing them away from the wall.

STRAWBERRY

| C | cool | none | mound | spring |

Ideal for the cold greenhouse. The plants give an early supply of fruit and only take up greenhouse space from late winter to early spring.

GROWING Use new plants growing in 13cm/5in pots filled with John Innes No 2. Leave outdoors for the first part of winter, choosing a cold spot where the roots will get a good chilling. In mid-winter move them onto the greenhouse staging away from slugs and mice. As the plants start growing, begin watering and feeding with a general-purpose liquid feed. Beware of overwatering which rots the roots. Pollinate the flowers by hand in the absence of any insects and shade the emerging fruit from the fiercest sunlight. Good ventilation is essential on the hottest days. As the fruit significantly swell increase the amount of liquid feed. Plant out afterwards.

HARVESTING The best picking time varies according to variety. Flavour peaks with some fruit when the top half of the berry is red and the bottom tip cream coloured. Wait until the entire strawberry is bright red with others.

VARIETIES 'Cambridge Favourite'; 'Royal Sovereign'.

POSSIBLE PROBLEMS Avoid using the same forced plant two years running since fruit quality deteriorates.

Tomato

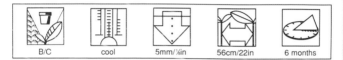

| B/C | cool | 5mm/¼in | 56cm/22in | 6 months |

Since tomatoes have an intense dislike of the cold they provide far better quality fruit under glass. But in the greenhouse they're pretty demanding and require constant pampering. Bush tomatoes require less effort, but they flop all over the place and are really for outdoors.

GROWING Either sow early spring in a heated propagator providing seeds with a temperature of 18°C/65°F, or wait until there's a hot week in early spring. Germination takes less than a fortnight under a fine covering of vermiculite. When the seedlings develop, thin to the strongest and plant up to a 7.5cm/3in pot. Leave until the first flowers appear (when the plant is some 20cm/8in tall) and then transfer to a grow-bag, bed, or 23cm/9in pot filled with John Innes No 3. Water sparingly to avoid plant wilt, and add a liquid tomato feed. As the fruit appear, so both can be increased. Snap off side shoots growing in the leaf axils, and when the fourth truss of fruit has set, stop the main growing point. Grow up a cane or a taut piece of string wedged under the plant's root system at one end, and tied to the greenhouse roof at the other.

HARVESTING By mid-summer when the plant is 1.5m/5ft tall the first crop will be ripening.

POSSIBLE PROBLEMS Look out for bright yellow or dark green marks on the fruit which are caused by an absence of potash and/or nitrogen, roasting temperatures, and sunburn. Cure by increasing ventilation and watering.

BEGONIA

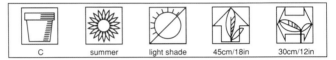

| C | summer | light shade | 45cm/18in | 30cm/12in |

There are three principal kinds of begonia, the fibrous, the rhizomatous, and tuberous hybrids *(above)*. The latter subdivide into pendulas, cascades, multiflora, and the single-flowering, all of which descend from a handful of colourful South American and Andean species.

GROWING Buy plants in late spring and start the tubers into growth on a warm windowsill. Lay them hollow side up on a tray of moist potting compost. When the shoots appear after four weeks pot each tuber into a 13cm/5in pot, with the tip of the tuber just above the compost surface. Keep in light shade over summer. For show-quality blooms remove the female flowers which are smaller than the large male. Water and feed well. Towards the end of summer, as the leaves yellow, reduce the amount of watering. The flower stems will fall off. Over winter the tuber should be kept in a frost-free place.

PROPAGATION Increase by seed in early spring. Sow thinly and cover with sand. Cover the pot with glass and raise at 18°C/65°F. Transplant seedlings into 2.5cm/1in pots. Alternatively take leaf cuttings.

VARIETIES Tuberous begonias: 'Apricot Delight' has peach flowers; 'Goliath', red; 'Goldilocks', yellow; 'Hawaii', orange; 'Icicle', white; 'Sugar Candy', pink.

POSSIBLE PROBLEMS Aphids; mildew; vine weevil.

CALCEOLARIA

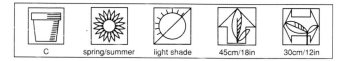

| C | spring/summer | light shade | 45cm/18in | 30cm/12in |

The most magical calceolaria have puffed-up, bloated flowers in gaudy colours; sulphur-yellow, blood-red and orange, sometimes with a liberal dash of spots.

GROWING They divide into shrubby and herbaceous kinds. The former are tall specimens and flower for several months. The latter have huge blotched heads, with bright flowers. Shrubby calceolaria will flower profusely in a 15cm/6in pot with John Innes No 2. Induce bushiness by occasionally pinching out. Herbaceous kinds are usually grown from seed *(see below)*. For all calceolaria keep the soil moist and plant in a light, airy position.

PROPAGATION Sow seeds in seed compost and maintain at 18°C/65°F. When large enough to handle pot up singly into a 12.5cm/5in pot with John Innes No 1.

SPECIES *C.* × *herbeohybrida (above)* has a number of varieties all equally eye-catching. Shades of red, yellow, and orange scream for attention. They tend to be 45cm/18in tall, though there is a dwarf strain, Multiflora Nana, at half the height.

POSSIBLE PROBLEMS Whitefly can be a major nuisance; also leafhoppers.

CAMPANULA

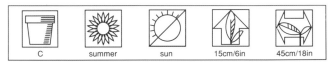

C	summer	sun	15cm/6in	45cm/18in

The most popular greenhouse campanula is *C. isophylla* *(above)*, the Italian bellflower. It has trailing, green-grey, heart-shaped leaves and is available with white or blue flowers. It makes a lively hanging basket.

GROWING Grow in a 13cm/5in pot or hanging basket filled with John Innes No 2. Provide a relatively cool position since it dislikes hot, dry conditions. Keep the soil moist over spring and summer; conversely do not overwater. After flowering, trim back the plant and keep on the dry side through winter at a minimum of 7°C/45°F. The basket can be hung outdoors over summer, but for the best display definitely keep in the greenhouse.

PROPAGATION Take three cuttings 5cm/2in long in mid-spring. Insert in a 9cm/3½in pot filled with loam-based seed compost with a good scattering of fine sand. Campanula rarely fails to take root.

SPECIES As an alternative try growing *C. pyramidalis*, the chimney bellflower, in a pot. It reaches a height of 1.2m/4ft and flowers in late spring. *C. i.* has an attractive variety, 'Mayi', with woolly, variegated leaves.

POSSIBLE PROBLEMS Aphids can be a major nuisance.

CINERARIA

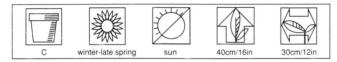

| C | winter-late spring | sun | 40cm/16in | 30cm/12in |

Highly attractive winter- and spring-flowering plants, with large single daisy-like blooms in a wide range of colours. Plants are usually on sale from autumn, and last for two months under glass, rather less indoors.

GROWING Treat as biennials, sow this year to flower next, and then discard. Keep mature plants in John Innes No 2 in 17cm/7in pots at approximately 13°C/55°F. As the flower buds swell the temperature can be raised to 16°C/61°F, when feeding commences. Reduce the temperature slightly, as the buds open, and the flowers will last considerably longer.

PROPAGATION Sow the seed from late spring for a Christmas display. Cover the pots with glass and keep moist until they germinate. When four leaves have formed, pot up the strongest seedlings. Gradually move into 11cm/4½in pots using a peat-based soil.

VARIETIES *C. cruenta* 'Spring Glory' has showy white flowers with a pink outer ring and centre. Other kinds, under the name *Senecio* × *hybridus*, come in small and large flowering sizes, in a wide colour range.

POSSIBLE PROBLEMS Greenfly; overwatering.

GRAPE

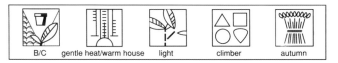

B/C	gentle heat/warm house	light	climber	autumn

To avoid a vine taking over the greenhouse roof, restrict size of certain varieties by growing as a 1.2m/4ft high container standard.

GROWING Insert good drainage material in the soil and prepare wires running the length of the roof for tying-in. In spring prune the vine to 15cm/6in above the soil, cutting just above a leaf joint. Select the three most vigorous new shoots and remove the rest. On reaching 1.5m/5ft high pinch out the growing tips and allow new side shoots to develop three leaves before pinching out. This pruning programme is vital for creating a strong framework. During the growing period water well with a liquid fertilizer, reducing both when the autumn foliage falls. Every winter cut back each stem to 20cm/8in from the main trunk. From the second year on let the leading buds grow unhindered, unless growth is too prolific. Although flowers and fruit will develop in the second year, there won't be a decent crop until the third.

POSSIBLE PROBLEMS Lack of ventilation and high humidity lead to mildew.

VARIETIES Black grapes: 'Lady Hastings' (early); 'Black Hamburgh' (mid-season); 'West's St. Peter's' (late). White grapes: 'Royal Muscadine' (early); 'Muscat of Hungary' (mid-season); 'Golden Queen' (late).

JASMINUM

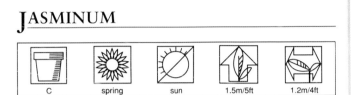

| C | spring | sun | 1.5m/5ft | 1.2m/4ft |

J. polyanthum (above) is one of the most highly scented indoor plants. It comes from China and can be treated as a 1.5m/5ft climber if given a 30cm/12in pot. In a smaller container, with sensible pruning, it can be kept to more manageable proportions.

GROWING Provide plenty of light. Garden-centre plants often have their stems too closely wrapped round each other. If so, unravel immediately before the task becomes too tricky, and train up and around canes. After flowering in spring cut back to generate new, flowering growth. Over summer stand outside in dappled shade and regularly feed (with additional potash). Bring back under glass in mid-autumn and decrease the amount of watering. Generally, it is better to let the leaves wilt slightly and tell you when water is required rather than to overwater. The cooler the winter/spring temperatures the later will be the flowering.

PROPAGATION Take 10cm/4in heel cuttings in spring or autumn and plant up in a sand/peat mix. Raise at 18°C/65°F over winter and subsequently grow in John Innes No 2.

SPECIES *J. rex* needs higher tropical temperatures and, despite being capable of a much longer flowering period than *J. polyanthum*, is totally scentless.

POSSIBLE PROBLEMS New growth attracts aphids.

LILIUM

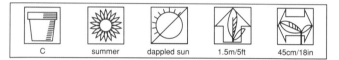

| C | summer | dappled sun | 1.5m/5ft | 45cm/18in |

Lilies can be grown in pots or borders. Pots give you greater control over their sometimes fussy growing conditions; you can also move them about, particularly the highly scented. The disadvantage is the extra work. A sane compromise is three extravagant pots.

GROWING In spring, plant three bulbs into a 30cm/12in, deeper-than-average pot. Stem-rooters go in slightly deeper than base-rooting bulbs. Use John Innes No 2, with plenty of horticultural grit and peat, and a thick bottom layer of crocks. First-rate drainage is absolutely essential. Sit the bulbs on a scattering of sharp sand and moisten the soil. Keep in a cool place and when the shoots appear move into the open during the day, but bring under cover while there's still the likelihood of frost. In summer keep the flowers and foliage in the sun, the roots in cooler shade. Let the foliage die down and reduce watering.

PROPAGATION Remove offsets after flowering.

SPECIES For scent; *L. auratum (above)*, white with yellow stripes, though it can be tricky to grow; *L. regale*, white with yellow throat; *L.* 'Pink Perfection', pink; *L.* 'Star Gazer', rosy-red with crimson spots. Unscented; *L.* 'Milano', orange; *L.* 'Yellow Star', golden yellow.

POSSIBLE PROBLEMS Aphids; basal rot; leatherjackets.

MAMMILLARIA

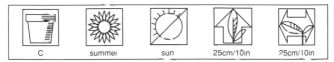

C	summer	sun	25cm/10in	25cm/10in

Highly popular cacti which are reliable, prolific flowerers. Shapes tend to be vertical and spherical, with attractive spines.

GROWING Place in a bright place throughout the year, and water carefully. In winter cease watering altogether, in spring water gently, and in summer let the soil dry between liberal applications. The soil, John Innes No 2, should have a 40 per cent addition of horticultural grit to improve drainage. The flowers are mainly white or red, the latter generally appearing later than the former.

PROPAGATION Slice away offsets from the parent in summer and pot up in a mix of four parts John Innes No 1, one part fine sand. Seed germinates at 20°C/68°F. When large enough to handle pot up into 7.5cm/3in pots of John Innes No 2.

SPECIES *M. elegans* send up a long stem with red flowers. *M. erythrosperma* is like a green pin-cushion; cherry-red flowers followed by fruit. *M. sempervivi* has yellow flowers; *M. theresae,* violet-purple flowers; *M. zeilmanniana (above)*, purple flowers.

POSSIBLE PROBLEMS Mealy bugs.

43

PELARGONIUM

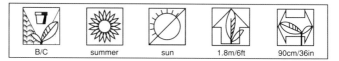

| B/C | summer | sun | 1.8m/6ft | 90cm/36in |

These are not hardy herbaceous geranium but tender, invariably South African plants which survive most maltreatment, except overwatering. This is fatal. The range of plants is huge and increasing annually. Many have scented leaves. It's well worth visiting a national collection to see the latest forms.

GROWING Repot in spring with John Innes No 2, horticultural grit and bottom crocks for good drainage. Pelargoniums can withstand dry soil but not waterlogging which rots the roots. Feed fortnightly over summer and pinch back to increase extra growth. If placing pots of ivy-leaf geranium outdoors, note that heavy downfalls can easily bend and break off the fragile stems. Main branches should be supported and tied in.

PROPAGATION Take cuttings of new growth in summer and root in John Innes No 1. Only when the 5cm/2in pot is root-bound should you pot up.

SPECIES The three major categories are ivy-leaved, regal, and zonal *(above)*, though specialist nurseries offer further kinds. 'Scarlet Unique' is a splendid multi-branching shrub with bright red flowers flecked black. 'Jacky Gould' and 'Rio Grande' (both ivy) are a good mix with papery white, rose-like petals, and red-black.

POSSIBLE PROBLEMS Whitefly.

PRIMULA

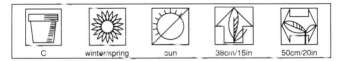

| C | winter/spring | sun | 38cm/15in | 50cm/20in |

Many greenhouse primula are natives of China and need winter temperatures of 13°C/55°F. They range in size from the large flowering to the dainty, and are extremely good value.

GROWING Use 13cm/5in pots filled with John Innes No 2 and with good bottom drainage. Keep cool and well-watered while in flower, with some humidity and good light, but out of direct sunlight.

PROPAGATION Germinate seed at 18°C/65°F in early spring. Cover the seed tray with a sheet of glass and remove when seedlings appear. Gradually pot up to 13cm/5in containers, and harden off over summer in a cold frame but again out of direct sunlight. Bring back under glass in mid-autumn and feed with a potash-high fertilizer until the buds begin to open. These primula do not last long (at best several years) and are eventually discarded. Raise fresh stock every other year from seed.

SPECIES *P. × kewensis* has clusters of bright yellow flowers and a long flowering season. It should last a few years unlike the scented annual *P. malacoides* which comes in various colours, mainly reds, violets, and white. *P. obconica* and *P. sinensis* are equally worth growing.

POSSIBLE PROBLEMS Beware aphids and botrytis in badly ventilated greenhouses.

ANTIRRHINUM

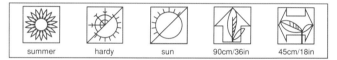

| summer | hardy | sun | 90cm/36in | 45cm/18in |

Tall antirrhinum (*A. majus* – hardy annuals) are ideal for the middle row of the border. They've got height, are supported by surrounding plants, and have long stems of flower that last up to the first frost. Squeeze the flowers and they look like the open jaws of a dragon, hence the common name, snapdragon.

PROPAGATION Early spring-sown seed (at 18°C/65°F) produces plants for hardening off three months later and setting out shortly after. They like rich, quick-draining soil in an open sunny position. Pinch out when 10cm/4in high for extra side growth unless you want cut flowers, in which case leave single stems. Deadhead right through summer. Antirrhinum can also be grown as pot plants with four per 30cm/12in container. For early flowering sow in mid-summer, harden off outside in the autumn, and bring back under glass as the temperature cools down.

VARIETIES There are three groups categorized by size. Tall (60cm/24in and over) – 'Bright Butterfly', 'Coronette', and the series 'Supreme'. Medium (30-60cm/12-24in) – 'Madame Butterfly', 'His Excellency', and the Monarch series. Low (up to 30cm/12in) – 'Little Darling', 'Little Gem Mixed', and 'Pixie'.

POSSIBLE PROBLEMS Mildew causes stunted growth. Rust creates dark brown leaf pustules. Aphids.

Azalea

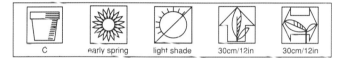

| C | early spring | light shade | 30cm/12in | 30cm/12in |

Greenhouse azaleas are far trickier to grow than outdoor kinds, but they give a sensational flowering display. Excellent as late winter gifts.

GROWING Provide a steady temperature of 16°C/61°F, with moist, shady conditions. After flowering, deadhead and spray against botrytis. In mid-spring pot up using only lime-free compost otherwise you'll kill the plant, and give the occasional liquid feed. Only use rain or cold, boiled water. Increase ventilation, and from early summer to mid-autumn plunge the pot outside in a sheltered shady bed so its rim is level with the ground. Keep the soil moist. Return the pot to the greenhouse in autumn and wait for the next crop of flower buds.

PROPAGATION This is a job for the professionals. You can try grafting or taking cuttings but it is a slow, precise science and generally not worth attempting.

SPECIES The choice is limited but the many varieties of *Rhododendron simsii* (Indian azalea; *above*) are very suitable for growing in the greenhouse.

POSSIBLE PROBLEMS Watch out for aphids, they can be quite a nuisance.

47

CALADIUM

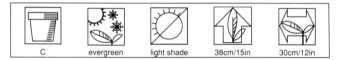

| C | evergreen | light shade | 38cm/15in | 30cm/12in |

Caladium are greenhouse tuberous perennials which unfold spectacular, brightly patterned leaves. *C. × hortulanum*, angel's wings, is top of the range with creamy-white centres, mottled green edging, and crimson veining.

GROWING Start the tubers into growth in early spring at 21°C/70°F. Place in a box of moist peat and, when growth begins, pot into a small container filled with John Innes No 2. Provide a thick layer of drainage material at the bottom. When the leaves begin to appear water freely and increase the humidity. In mid-summer give a regular liquid feed. Decrease both feed and water as the foliage fades in the autumn, and store the tuber in a frost-free room at approximately 13°C/55°F, gently wetting the soil occasionally.

PROPAGATION In spring carefully remove new offsets from the parent tuber. Pot up singly as described above.

VARIETIES *C. bicolor (above)*: 'Pink Cloud' has pink mottling in the leaf centre with whitish veins. 'Pink Beauty' has similar pink mottling but with pink-purple veins; and 'John Peed' has bright rusty centres and crimson veining.

POSSIBLE PROBLEMS Generally trouble-free.

CLIVIA

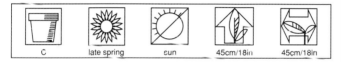

| C | late spring | sun | 45cm/18in | 45cm/18in |

Clivia make excellent choices for rich spring colour. A robust plant can easily produce 40 or more flowers, with different varieties offering bright orange, red and yellow blooms.

GROWING Plant up in 15cm/6in pots filled with John Innes No 2. Be careful with the watering. Over winter make sure the soil doesn't dry out, and through the growing period do not water too liberally. All container-grown specimens must sit above a good layer of drainage material so the roots don't stand in wet soil. The plant will need to be in a 30cm/12in pot within a couple of years .

PROPAGATION To prevent potting up into ever larger containers remove a pot-bound specimen and divide. Transplant the new growth into 10cm/4in pots filled with John Innes No 1.

SPECIES *C. miniata (above)* produces 15 dark orange flowers per stem set against deep green foliage. For variegated leaves chose *C. m.* 'Striata'. *C. nobilis*'s flowers are more of a fiery orange red.

POSSIBLE PROBLEMS Mealy bugs are the main problem.

CYCLAMEN

| C | spring | semi-shade | 20cm/8in | 20cm/8in |

C. persicum (above) is the plant for the greenhouse. It has a light scent – lily-of-the-valley to some, intoxicating, stale cardboard to others – and flowers like Flemish hats. Each has five, white, vertical twisted petals, with a crimson ring at the base. The foliage has ornate mottling of dark and pale green. The florist's cyclamen is scentless but has larger flowers.

GROWING Plant *C. p.*'s corm in a 15cm/6in pot filled with John Innes No 1 and plenty of drainage material. Give good ventilation over summer (eg a cold frame) and little watering. Cease altogether in mid-summer when there's no new foliage. In late summer pot up, with the top edge of the corm just visible above the soil. Commence watering and bring under glass in autumn, maintaining a temperature of at least 10°C/50°F.

PROPAGATION Since the corms will not divide, increase by seeds sown in winter at 16°C/61°F. Water sensibly because too little or too much can be fatal. Pot up into 6cm/2½in pots.

VARIETIES *C. p.* 'Silberstrahl'; *C. p.* 'Rex' has green and bright white mottled leaves.

POSSIBLE PROBLEMS Vine weevil; botrytis.

CYMBIDIUM

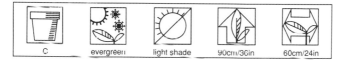

| C | evergreen | light shade | 90cm/36in | 60cm/24in |

Cymbidium are graceful, evergreen, epiphytic orchids. Most of them originate from the Far East and Australia.

GROWING If growing in a pot use special orchid compost consisting of bark, loam, and spagnum moss. Plant in a 12.5cm/5in container with plenty of drainage material and pot up in alternate years. Cymbidium can reach a huge size needing 50cm/20in containers. Provide continuous humidity, never letting the atmosphere dry out.

PROPAGATION Increase by division in spring. Each section should have roots and top growth. Water in after one week.

SPECIES *C. Pontac* 'Mont Millais' flowers in spring with layers of dark red and white petals; *C. devonianum* has green and purple flowers, and blooms in summer. *C. grandiflorum* has brown spots and green flowers, and blooms in winter.

POSSIBLE PROBLEMS Scale insects; aphids; red spider mite; leaf discolouration.

DATURA

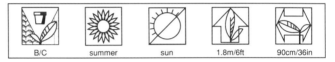

| B/C | summer | sun | 1.8m/6ft | 90cm/36in |

Datura reach 10m/35ft trees in the wild, sensationally covered in large trumpet-like flowers which give off the headiest scent imaginable. The leaves are hallucinogenic if eaten and cause prolonged outbreaks of vomiting.

GROWING Daturas, or angels trumpets, are vigorous growers. Plant up only to the next size pot, and only when root-bound move up again. Try to limit its growth and height because if you plant straight into a 30cm/12in container the roots will quickly fill it. Use John Innes No 2 initially, and thereafter No 3, and water freely over summer. As the flower buds begin to swell in mid-summer feed with tomato fertilizer. After flowering in the autumn cut back by a third, which also helps to eradicate pests. In a large pot you restrict size to 1.8m/6ft.

PROPAGATION Increase easily by seed. Sow at 18°C/65°F and pot up seedlings into 7.5cm/3in pots. Alternatively, take cuttings of semi-ripe wood in late spring and plant up at 21°C/70°F.

SPECIES *D. arborea* (listed as *Brugmansia aurea*) has white flowers 25cm/10in long, while those of *B. suaveolens* are pale yellow. *D. inoxia* (*D. meteloides*) is the most fragrant of all. For colour chose the apricot *D.* 'Grand Marnier'.

POSSIBLE PROBLEMS Red spider mite; whitefly.

EUPHORBIA

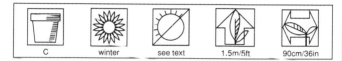

| C | winter | see text | 1.5m/5ft | 90cm/36in |

The most popular greenhouse euphorbia is *E. pulcherrima* (*above*) or the poinsettia, a brash and tricky plant. It has striking red bracts but won't easily repeat this showy performance a second year.

GROWING Keep at approximately 18°C/65°F. When the bracts have died down cut back the plant almost to the base, and reduce watering so the soil is virtually dry. In early summer kick-start it into life with fresh compost and water. Feed regularly and for the next two months provide a minimum of 14-hours darkness per day. When the new bracts start to colour you can put an end to this regime. Those successful in keeping a poinsettia going should note that it will get bigger year by year and could reach a maximum height of approximately 1.5m/5ft.

PROPAGATION After pruning, use new shoots as cuttings.

SPECIES There are 2000 species of euphorbia. *E. fulgens* is one of the most similar to poinsettia and has smaller scarlet bracts.

POSSIBLE PROBLEMS The main danger is not giving the correct number of hours of darkness. This is absolutely crucial.

HIPPEASTRUM

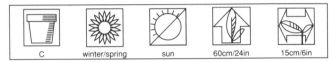

| C | winter/spring | sun | 60cm/24in | 15cm/6in |

Hippeastrum, or amaryllis as it is popularly known, is a vigorous flowering bulb. For very little effort you get a tall, showy display in the first part of the year. Most bulb specialists will have at least 15 varieties to chose from, including one or two with scent.

GROWING In spring plant the bulb half-in and half-out of John Innes No 2. Use a pot just 5cm/2in wider than the bulb's diameter, with plenty of drainage material in the bottom. Wet the soil initially, only increasing the amounts as the temperature rises from 13°C/55°F and growth develops. Delay feeding until two weeks before flowering, but continue thereafter every 10 days until the foliage turns yellow and begins to die. Rest the bulb from late autumn and start it into growth again when it suits you, even as early as late winter. Repot with fresh compost.

PROPAGATION Sow seed in the spring at 18°C/65°F, but avoid resting the growing plants.

VARIETIES 'Apple Blossom' is white and pink, and has mild scent. 'Bouquet' is light pink. 'Yellow Pioneer' is yellow.

POSSIBLE PROBLEMS Mealy bugs; tarsonemid mite; thrips.

HOYA

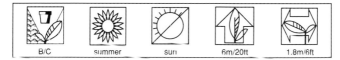

| B/C | summer | sun | 6m/20ft | 1.8m/6ft |

A tall evergreen climber whose size, and therefore flowering capacity, can be restricted by growing it in a medium-size pot. Given free growth it produces masses of waxy, white, star-like flowers each with a red centre. Highly scented nectar.

GROWING Use John Innes No 2 and train against a trellis up and under the greenhouse roof, like a vine. Good light and sun are essential, as is reasonable humidity. Spray twice daily. Let the soil dry a little between waterings, and keep much drier over winter. Severe temperature fluctuations lead to bud and leaf drop. Deadhead for a continuous flowering display.

PROPAGATION Increase by stem cuttings in early summer, each retaining three pairs of leaves.

SPECIES *H. bella* grows to 45cm/18in and is ideal for a hanging basket. *H. carnosa (above)* reaches 6m/20ft. If space is limited use a 15cm/6in pot; better still grow in a 30cm/12in pot; ideally raise in a bed. The scent is generally strongest in the evening.

POSSIBLE PROBLEMS Overwatering and lack of flower buds due to insufficient feeding.

IPOMOEA

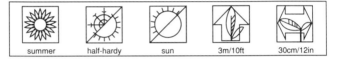

| summer | half-hardy | sun | 3m/10ft | 30cm/12in |

Three species are grown as annuals including *I. purpurea*, morning glory (so named because the purple flowers are at their glorious best early in the day, and fade with the afternoon). Though these climbers can be grown outside in a warm bed, they also make exceptional plants for ornamental pots.

PROPAGATION Germinate the seeds in mid-spring at a minimum of 15°C/60°F or the seedling will gradually die. Transplant two young plants to an 7.5cm/3in pot filled with John Innes No 1, pinch out, and later transfer to a 20cm/8in pot with John Innes No 2. Stand against a trellis so the growth can be tied in. Outside, plant in a free-draining, rich soil against a warm, sunny wall for support.

SPECIES Half-hardy annuals: *I. coccinea* has scented, scarlet flowers (height 3m/10ft); *I. purpurea* grows to 3m/10ft; *I. quamoclit* has orange flowers (height 1.8m/6ft), *I. tricolor* (*above*) has purple-blue flowers (height 2.4m/8ft). Perennials are also available: *I. lobata* syn. *Mina lobata* is so tender it's often grown as an annual. The same is true of *I. violacea* which has lilac flowers (height 2.4m/8ft).

POSSIBLE PROBLEMS Aphids attack the tender young shoots.

LATHYRUS

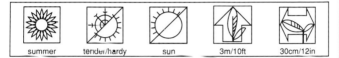

| summer | tender/hardy | sun | 3m/10ft | 30cm/12in |

Modern varieties of *L. odoratus (above)*, the sweet pea, feature colour and size at the expense of scent. But the older kinds are still available. There's a great deal of conflicting advice about the best way to grow sweet pea. The latest research goes as follows.

PROPAGATION Show specimens for mild-climate gardens can be sown in situ in the autumn. For cottage garden displays, and colder areas, sow in the spring under glass. Before planting quickly rub the seeds on a sheet of sandpaper to let water in and speed up germination. Next, fill a small but deep peat pot with John Innes No 1, water, and plant three seeds. Raise at 15°C/60°F and thin to the strongest shoot in each pot. Gradually harden off in a sunny position and then plant out. For prize specimens remove all tendrils and side growth, concentrating the plant's energy on its bloom. Tie in to a stake. In all other cases leave the tendrils which attach themselves to fences, etc. A wigwam of canes saves space.

SPECIES *L. odoratus* has many different varieties including dwarf (height from 45cm/18in to 1.2m/4ft), and giant (3m/10ft). Two everlasting, perennial sweet peas are *L. latifolius* and *L. rotundifolius*.

POSSIBLE PROBLEMS Aphids; mildew; slugs.

LOBELIA

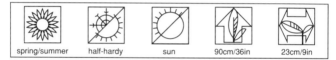

| spring/summer | half-hardy | sun | 90cm/36in | 23cm/9in |

Trailing lobelia are traditionally reserved for the hanging basket, though they look equally good at the front of the border flowering hither and thither among other plants. Tall and small kinds come in a wide range of sharp colours. *L. erinus* (height 15cm/6in), and *L. tenuior* (height 30cm/12in) are both perennials grown as annuals.

PROPAGATION Germinate seeds in early spring at 18°C/65°F. Thin down to the most vigorous shoots, reduce the temperature, and harden off in late spring. A continuous sowing and regular deadheading gives a long summer's display.

SPECIES The compact varieties of *L. erinus* include: 'Cambridge Blue', 'Mrs Clibran', and 'Snowball'. Trailing varieties: 'Red Cascade', and 'Sapphire'. *L. tenuior* is particularly suitable for winter-flowering pots. Other perennials include *L. fulgens* and *L. siphilitica*, both of which grow to 90cm/36in. *L. × vedrariense (above)*, grows slightly higher.

POSSIBLE PROBLEMS Damping off and stem rot makes the plants wilt and eventually collapse.

NICOTIANA

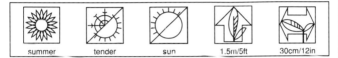

| summer | tender | sun | 1.5m/5ft | 30cm/12in |

The paler varieties of the tobacco plant invariably have the strongest, heady fragrance which is released in the evenings. The tallest species is *N. sylvestris* from the Andean foothills which grows to 1.5m/5ft. It's said to be coarse looking, but the scent is strong enough to fill the greenhouse. It can also be grown in a pot and brought indoors after sunset. The genus owes its common name to *N. tabacum* whose leaves are used in the tobacco industry.

PROPAGATION Germinate seed in early spring at a temperature of 18°C/65°F. Prick off the most vigorous seedlings and pot up in containers using John Innes No 2. The tallest varieties need staking, though *N. sylvestris* is quite sturdy. Water liberally and shelter from fierce sunlight.

SPECIES *N. alata (above)*, is a half-hardy annual which will survive a mild winter, though it gets a bit straggly and is best replaced by spring plants; height 75cm/30in. *N. suaveolens*, also an annual, is smaller at 1m/3ft 3in and makes a good pot plant.

POSSIBLE PROBLEMS Aphids attack the young growth.

ORANGE

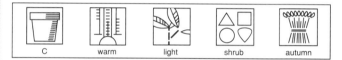

C	warm	light	shrub	autumn

Three basic kinds are available – sweet oranges *(Citrus sinensis)*, bitter *(C. aurantium)*, and mandarin *(C. nobilis deliciosa)*. Within each group are a number of juicy varieties. The best choices for beginners are 'Malta Blood' (sweet), 'Chinotto' (bitter), and 'Satsuma' (mandarin). Height 1.2m/4ft x 1.2m/4ft.

GROWING Follow the same method as for lemon, buying and potting up a young shrub or grow from a pip. Sow just under a layer of John Innes No 1 in early spring and maintain at 21°C/70°F. Germination varies from a fortnight to one month. When the seedling is large enough to handle, move into a 7.5cm/3in pot and maintain at the same temperature. When the orange eventually develops into a young shrub prune in early spring if you want to restrict size. The plant will withstand a severe reduction every other year.

HARVESTING Although citrus plants are quite tough and can survive most frost-free temperatures, they need constant warmth (minimum 10°C/50°F) to produce fruit.

POSSIBLE PROBLEMS When mealy bugs or scale insects strike they leave behind a sticky substance which in turn attracts sooty mould. Spray to kill the insects and either wipe off the mould or, in severe cases, cut back the affected areas.

PETUNIA

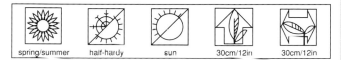

spring/summer   half-hardy   sun   30cm/12in   30cm/12in

The blue and purple petunias have the best evening scent. The genus thrives in good summers, and is traditionally grown in all kinds of ornamental containers from hanging baskets to free-standing chimney pots, but can be ruined by a chilly wet season. 'Resisto Mixed' is the best strain for withstanding bad weather on exposed sites.

PROPAGATION Germinate seeds in early spring at 15°C/60°F and harden off seedlings before setting out. Plant in light soil in full sun. Too rich a soil in too dark a situation results in foliage instead of flowers. For pot plants use John Innes No 1.

VARIETIES There are four groups. Multifloras are bushy prodigious flowerers and include scores of F_1 hybrids like 'Blue Skies' (light blue) and 'Bumble' (ginger). Grandifloras have larger, fewer flowers. They include 'Californian Girl' (yolk-yellow) and 'Razzle-Dazzle' (in various colours). The final two groups are Nana Compacta (15cm/6in high), and Pendula whose trailing stems are ideal for hanging baskets.

POSSIBLE PROBLEMS Aphids feed on the tender young shoots.

61

SAINTPAULIA

| C | mainly summer | light shade | 12.5cm/5in | 23cm/9in |

The African violet, *S. ionantha*, forms a compact rosette of fleshy, hairy leaves out of which flowers appear in a good, strong range of colours. They appear all summer, and often throughout the year.

GROWING Raise in small pots, rarely bigger than 12.5cm/ 5in, using a peat-based compost. Only water – always from below – when the soil is getting dry, and wipe off any splashes that get on the leaves. This quickly leads to discolouration. Also avoid direct, scorching sunlight. To provide local humidity stand the pot on a tray packed with pebbles and half-filled with water. Over summer feed with weak applications of tomato fertilizer. At 18°C/65°F they should flower freely from summer to autumn, if not beyond.

PROPAGATION Select a mature leaf and cut it off cleanly at the base. Shorten the stem to 4cm/1¾in and dip into rooting powder. Plant in John Innes No 1 leaving a small space between the leaf and the soil surface. It should root in eight weeks.

VARIETIES 'Fancy Pants' has white flowers, edged red. 'Rhapsody' is purple. 'Willy Wilkins' is pink.

POSSIBLE PROBLEMS Tarsonemid mites.

SANSEVIERIA

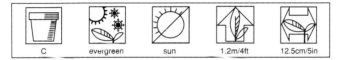

| C | evergreen | sun | 1.2m/4ft | 12.5cm/5in |

The most popular species is *S. trifasciata*, mother-in-law's tongue, *(above)*, so named because of the astonishingly long, vertical, indestructible, variegated, wagging, tongue-like leaves.

GROWING Since the plant grows slowly it rarely needs repotting. Use a 15cm/6in pot filled with John Innes No 2 and place in full light to bring out the lime green/yellow edge to the foliage. In the winter if you maintain a temperature of 13°C/55°F, water and allow the soil to dry out between applications. It will certainly tolerate 10°C/50°F if it is kept dry. Give a weak, monthly feed over summer. The plant sometimes produces a green/white summer flower.

PROPAGATION Increase by offsets when they are 10cm/4in tall. Ease them away and pot up in the smallest size container appropriate. Water sparingly at first.

VARIETIES *S. t.* 'Golden Hahnii' has a rosette of dark green leaves, each with broad yellowish borders (height 30cm/12in). 'Hahnii' also has a rosette but with mottled green foliage (height 30cm/12in). 'Laurentii' has vertical, 1.2m/4ft high erect leaves.

POSSIBLE PROBLEMS Brown blotches can appear on the foliage.

SENECIO

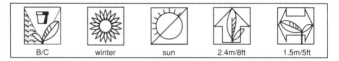

| B/C | winter | sun | 2.4m/8ft | 1.5m/5ft |

The senecio species for the greenhouse is *S. macroglossus* 'Variegatum' *(above)*. It's a climbing ivy with daisy-like flowers and a reddish stem, and is otherwise known as the wax vine. The pale yellow winter flowers complement the lime green leaf variegation.

GROWING Raise in John Innes No 2 and water sparingly in winter. It is quite tolerant of a warm, dry atmosphere though the occasional misting will greatly perk up the foliage and keep it clean. Growth is on the slow side and sometimes straggly, in which case pinch back for a more manageable, bushier plant.

PROPAGATION Take a 10cm/4in semi-ripe cutting in summer and plant up in John Innes No 1 with additional sharp sand for quick drainage. Pot up the following spring with John Innes No 2 either into a larger container or the greenhouse border.

VARIETIES *S. macroglossus* has plain, mid-green foliage.

POSSIBLE PROBLEMS Generally trouble-free.

STRELITZIA

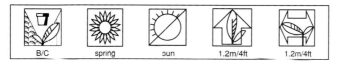

| B/C | spring | sun | 1.2m/4ft | 1.2m/4ft |

The exotic, intense colouring and flamboyant outline of the bird of paradise, *S. reginae (above)*, suggests it needs very special handling. Not so. In fact the only problem is size. Plants will not flower unless they're in the greenhouse border or a large pot, and easily grow to substantial 1.2m/4ft clumps.

GROWING Use a 30cm/12in pot filled with John Innes No 3 on a thick layer of drainage material. Water gently until the plant is established and maintain a temperature of 13°C/55°F. Increase watering in the summer and decrease over winter. On hot days ventilate, and protect the leaves from scorching sunshine.

PROPAGATION In spring divide mature plants, and raise in a more humid atmosphere at a temperature nearer 18°C/65°F. Alternatively, detach suckers and treat in the same way.

SPECIES *S. r.* is quite different from anything else. *S. nicolai* is a monstrous evergreen, with 1.5m/5ft leaves and a height of 6m/20ft. The flowers, if you can stretch to see them, are pale blue/white.

POSSIBLE PROBLEMS Scale insects.

AUBERGINE

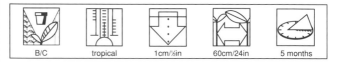

| B/C | tropical | 1cm/½in | 60cm/24in | 5 months |

Otherwise known as 'egg-plants', aubergines come in two colours, purple and white. The purple are excellent for Mediterranean type dishes, and the white for pickling.

GROWING Raise as an annual, sowing the particularly slow-growing seeds in spring at 21°C/70°F using John Innes No 1. Transfer the seedlings to 9cm/3½in pots when they're large enough to handle, and reduce the heat to 18°C/65°F. After three months proceed to plant up individually into 30-38cm/12-15in pots with John Innes No 2, or two plants per grow-bag. Alternatively, use the greenhouse border. Feed with a liquid tomato fertilizer and never allow the plant to dry out. The best policy is 'little and often'. Growing the plant up string or canes is not essential, though for the sake of tidiness the latter is useful, in which case three 1.2m/4ft lengths are ideal for tying-in. For a bushier specimen stop the growing tip when the plant is 15cm/6in high, and only allow six fruit per plant.

HARVESTING The fruit will be ready for picking from early autumn. Either pick the young aubergines regularly when they are just big enough to use, or allow a maximum of six decent size fruits per plant.

POSSIBLE PROBLEMS Look out for aphids, whitefly and particularly red spider mite.

CODIAEUM

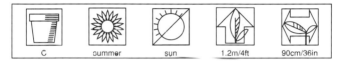

| C | summer | sun | 1.2m/4ft | 90cm/36in |

One of the few plants which needs to have its flowers automatically removed. They are not that attractive, and detract from the large, heavily veined, leathery, multicoloured leaves splashed in yellow-green-orange-red.

GROWING For the richest leaf colour give ample light, humid conditions and, crucially, steady temperatures. Fluctuations quickly lead to leaf drop. Also wipe the leaves to emphasize their glossiness. Start off young plants in 8cm/3in pots and move up to size 15cm/6in.

PROPAGATION The plants inevitably grow tall and leggy. When this happens cut back to encourage new growth lower down. The pruned tip sections (7.5cm/3in) can be used as cuttings. Cut off only the very bottom leaves so there will be foliage from the soil upward.

VARIETIES *C. variegatum* and *C. v. pictum (above)* both grow to 45cm/18in and have a wide range of colours.

POSSIBLE PROBLEMS Red spider mite; mealy bugs.

DIEFFENBACHIA

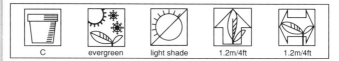

| C | evergreen | light shade | 1.2m/4ft | 1.2m/4ft |

Don't be fooled by the glossy, attractive foliage. Swallow the poisonous sap and you'll find it difficult to talk, hence the common names dumb cane, and the ironic mother-in-law. Nonetheless this is definitely worth growing and quite safe to handle.

GROWING Though dieffenbachia can be grown as a houseplant it succeeds best in greenhouses. Provide humidity for good leaf colour; water liberally over summer and sparingly in winter. If the leaves start to yellow increase the temperature.

PROPAGATION Detach suckers growing at the base and plant up in a mix of sand and peat. Alternatively, if the plant is getting too straggly, cut back and use 10cm/4in lengths of stem tip. These can also be grown by laying them in a tray of peat and sand at a temperature of 24°C/75°F. When they have developed a root system pot up in a 7.5cm/3in container.

SPECIES *D. maculata* and *D. m.* 'Exotica' have green and white, exuberantly mottled leaves. *D. picta* has similar patterning in lime green. *D. amoena (above)* has large, oblong shaped leaves.

POSSIBLE PROBLEMS Stem rotting if overwatered.

FITTONIA

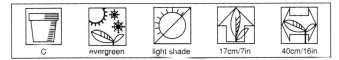

| C | evergreen | light shade | 17cm/7in | 40cm/16in |

Trailing plants with rich, ornamental foliage. *F. verschaffeltii* *(above)* has red-veined green foliage; *F. v.* 'Argyroneura' has slightly smaller leaves (10cm/4in) with white lines.

GROWING Provide a shaded position and good humidity. Don't let the winter temperature drop below 16°C/61°F and keep the compost dry in the dormant season. The plants generally decline rapidly with age and after a couple of seasons should be replaced by new specimens. They also tend to spread and scramble all over the place, in which case prune back to the new growth to maintain shape.

PROPAGATION Increase by removing offsets in late spring. Alternatively, divide the plant and retain fresh, vigorous growth while removing the tired centre.

SPECIES *F. gigantea* sometimes produces insignificant yellow flowers. *F. v.* 'Nana' is the small, compact version of *F. v.* 'Argyroneura'.

POSSIBLE PROBLEMS Generally trouble-free.

HIBISCUS

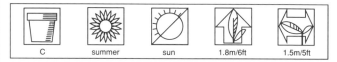

C	summer	sun	1.8m/6ft	1.5m/5ft

The Chinese rose, *H. rosa-sinensis (above)*, and particularly *H. r-s.* 'Cooperi', are the most suitable for the greenhouse. They have large, crimson, trumpet-like flowers, and without the root restrictions of a pot will quickly turn into a large shrub.

GROWING Hibiscus will eventually need a 30cm/12in pot filled with John Innes No 3. Keep a steady summer temperature of 18°C/65°F; any deviation leads to bud drop. Over winter provide a temperature of 16°C/61°F to avoid leaf drop. Prune in spring both to keep size under control and to prevent the base becoming bare and leggy. Good ventilation is necessary on the hottest summer days. Repot each spring.

PROPAGATION Take 10cm/4in heel cuttings in spring and raise in a sand and peat mix at 18°C/65°F. After rooting, pot up in John Innes No 2.

SPECIES *H. r-s.* 'Cooperi' has the more attractive foliage with green, creamy-white and red leaves. It is also better suited to smaller greenhouses since it can be grown in 15cm/6in pots.

POSSIBLE PROBLEMS Aphids; mealy bugs; red spider mite.

MELON

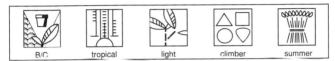

| B/C | tropical | light | climber | summer |

They are far more easily grown than is popularly believed. The one essential requirement is a 2.1m/7ft high greenhouse. Success is possible in a cold greenhouse but with artificial heat the results will be far better.

GROWING Sow seed in early spring for early/mid-summer fruit. Use 7.5cm/3in pots of seed compost covered with cling film. Remove when growth appears and provide a minimum temperature of 18°C/65°F. In the cold greenhouse sow seed inside a heated propagator, timing removal of the seedling to coincide with fine summer temperatures. The bed must be mounded to a height of 30cm/12in and fertilized with Growmore and a scattering of bonemeal. Provide vertical wire supports to the roof. Plant up, pinching out growing tips at 1.5m/5ft to encourage laterals which in turn must be stopped at five leaves. The resultant side shoots bear the fruit. Stop the latter growth at two leaves after the flowers, and limit each plant to five melons. Pollinate by hand and give adequate ventilation when temperatures exceed 23°C/73°F.

HARVESTING Press your finger tips into the top of the melon. When the fruit gently yields it is ripe.

POSSIBLE PROBLEMS Whitefly; red spider mite, mildew.

MONSTERA

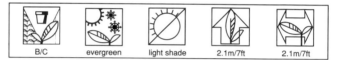

| B/C | evergreen | light shade | 2.1m/7ft | 2.1m/7ft |

The Mexican Swiss cheese plant makes a monstrous growth of glossy, indented foliage among a swirl of aerial roots grabbing at nearby vegetation for extra moisture. Impressive, and definitely not one for the smaller greenhouse.

GROWING Use John Innes No 3 and keep the soil moist over the growing season, dryish over winter. To prevent the aerial roots attacking other plants wrap together the former in wet moss. Particularly vigorous roots can be snipped off. Specimens grown in large pots (30cm/12in) or borders will need tying-in to stout stakes for support. High humidity is essential for abundant growth, good indentation, and the dramatic, pale orange flowering spathe (like corn-on-the cob) which only appears on established plants.

PROPAGATION Increase by side shoots which are teased away from the parent when they are 5cm/2in long. Pot up in a 13cm/5in pot filled with John Innes No 3.

SPECIES *M. deliciosa (above)* is the one for the greenhouse.

POSSIBLE PROBLEMS Generally trouble-free.

MUSHROOM

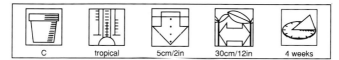

C	tropical	5cm/2in	30cm/12in	4 weeks

A mushroom's natural habitat is in the damp, dark corner of a meadow, and these are precisely the conditions for which you've got to aim.

GROWING It's possible to make your own mushroom compost but far easier to buy ready made. The former requires decomposing straw (created by giving it a regular watering and forking over) subjected to a drying out period at 60°C/140°F. With a kit you simply mix the mushroom spawn with the compost and store at 18°C/65°F in a shady spot. At all times avoid direct sunlight. Two weeks later when threads of mycelium appear through the compost you add the special covering layer provided, which promotes mushroom devel- opment. With the re-appearance of the mycelium begin to water lightly, and slightly reduce the temperature by a couple of degrees. The first mushroom should appear as a pinhead within three weeks.

HARVESTING Occurs about one week after the first pin-heads have been sighted. The initial crop tends to be the largest, though you should get three to five more.

POSSIBLE PROBLEMS Avoid overwatering which results in mushroom rot, and excessive dryness.

PESTS & DISEASES

PESTS

PROBLEM	DAMAGED CAUSED	REMEDY
Aphid (greenfly, blackfly)	Sap sucked; sticky honeydew on leaves	Spray leaves above and below with pirimicarb
Capsid bug	Leaf edges ragged, surface pitted with tiny holes	Spray with systemic insecticide
Caterpillar	Chewed-up stems, foliage, flowers	Spray with permethrin or trichlorphon
Eelworm	Weak plants with distorted stems and foliage	Destroy infected plants and discard compost
Leaf hopper	Sap sucked; white mottling/papery white cast-off skins on leaves	Spray with HETP or nicotine. Fumigate with nicotine under glass
Lily beetle	Chewed foliage	Spray with pirimphos-methyl
Mealy bug	Sap sucked; insect evident in white 'wool' covering	Spray with malathion
Red-spider mite	Sap sucked; yellow speckled foliage; brittle leaves	Spray with fenitrothion or malathion. Destroy badly affected plants
Root mealy bug	Root damaged; 'wool' on the inside of the pot	Spray with malathion
Scale insects	Sap sucked; yellow/brown scales on stems and leaf veins	Spray with methylated spirits or malathion
Sciarids	Small grey-black flies that run over top soil of plant pots or fly around them. Damage roots of seedlings and unhealthy plants	Spray with permethrin or malathion
Slugs and snails	Badly chewed-up foliage	Bury methiocarb just beneath soil surface in the border. Look for colonies inside empty pots
Thrips	Silver flecking on leaves and flowers	Spray with fenitrothion
Vine weevil	Entire plant wilts without visible explanation. Caused by black beetles attacking the root system	Discard plant; drench border soil with HCH
Whitefly	Sap sucked; flies clearly evident on foliage	Spray with permethrin
Wireworms	Roots eaten; fleshy seeds attacked	Fork in gamma-BHC

DISEASES

PROBLEM	DAMAGED CAUSED	REMEDY
Basal rot	Mainly affects lilies causing stunted growth and root decay	Dip the bulb in benomyl
Begonia tuber rot	Softening of the tuber skin rot	In future store in warmer, frost-free place
Botrytis (grey mould)	Grey fur covers stem and foliage	Immediately remove infected parts. Since botrytis affects damp, badly ventilated greenhouses improve conditions and spray with benomyl
Bud drop	Falling buds caused by too dry an atmosphere or soil, or overwatering	Increase/decrease the watering/humidity
Canker	Rough brown sunken area on stems	Cut out and burn; spray with thiophanate-methyl
Carnation wilt	Leaf yellowing	Destroy infected plants and sterilize the immediate growing area
Club root	Roots attacked, swelling occurs, unpleasant smell; may eventually lead to decay	Alkaline soil and a frequent sprinkling of lime. Water with solution of mercuric chloride or use calomel dust
Damping off	Fungi attacks seedlings causing them to wilt	Sow thinly and water carefully: drench with Chestnut compound
Leaf scorch	Discoloured foliage with brown blotches	Destroy affected areas and spray with zineb
Leaf spots	Brownish blotches and spots appear; leaves shrivel and drop	Spray with mancozeb
Neck rot	Attacks young melons and cucumbers, cacti and succulents	Avoid overwatering. With cacti remove affected parts, eg the top, and re-root
Oedema	Pimples or warts on the stalks. Outgrowths may become white powdery, blister or turn rusty-colour	Drier conditions in soil and air. Ventilate greenhouse; do not remove affected leaves
Powdery mildew	White powdery spots on foliage and sometimes stems	Fumigate with dinocap. Remove infected parts
Root rot	Plant wilt caused by overwatering	Transfer to new pot with dry compost and leave for two weeks before watering
Rust	Yellow speckling on upper leaf surface, orange pustules below	Spray with zineb; destroy infected parts; reduce greenhouse humidity

INDEX